BOOK ANALYSIS

By Benjamin Taylor

The Color Purple
by Alice Walker

Bright
≡Summaries.com

ALICE WALKER

AMERICAN NOVELIST AND ACTIVIST

- **Born in Georgia (USA) in 1944.**
- **Notable works:**
  - *The Third Life of Grange Copeland (1970)*, novel
  - *Meridian* (1976), novel
  - *In Search of our Mothers' Gardens* (1983), collected essays

Alice Walker was born the eighth child of two sharecroppers in Eatonton, Georgia in 1944. At the age of eight, she was involved in an accident involving a BB gun that left her blind in one eye. As a result, she grew to be more introverted, turning her attentions to reading and writing. She received a scholarship to Sarah Lawrence College in New York, and not long after graduating released the poetry collection *Once* (1968), her first published work in a career spanning 50 years and comprising numerous novels, poetry collections and essays. Her work is renowned for addressing issues related to race, gender and American history. She is also well known for her activism, championing racial and gender equality, and is credited as having coined the term 'womanism', a brand of feminism specific to the experiences of black women.

THE COLOR PURPLE

WRITING TO GOD

- **Genre:** novel.
- **Reference edition:** Walker, A. (1995) *The Color Purple*. London: The Women's Press Ltd.
- **1ˢᵗ edition:** 1982
- **Themes:** race, American society, sexuality, gender discrimination, female friendship, coming of age.

The Color Purple tells the story of Celie, a poor, uneducated African-American girl growing up in the early 20th-century American South. It is an epistolary novel, made up of letters written by Celie to God, and between Celie and her sister Nettie. It can be described as a Bildungsroman, a genre of novel that deals with coming-of-age and spiritual growth. Though the novel gained critical acclaim, winning both the 1983 Pulitzer Prize for Fiction and the National Book Award, it was criticised for what some believed to be negative and stereotypical portrayals of African-American men. It is nevertheless widely considered to be an important work of American, African-American and feminist literature, and has inspired successful film and stage adaptations.

SUMMARY

MARRIAGE TO MR

Celie writes a series of letters to God in a desperate bid to understand her situation. Alphonso, the man she thinks to be her father, rapes her repeatedly and impregnates her twice, taking both babies from her and giving them away to an unknown foster family. Soon after, Celie's mother dies, leaving her alone with Alphonso and her beloved younger sister Nettie, who is being courted by an older widower. However, Alphonso decides that Nettie is too young to marry, and instead Celie is married to the man, who is only ever referred to as 'Mr'.

One day, Celie recognises her daughter in town with a woman, who Celie identifies as the girl's foster mother. She questions the woman and discovers that she is married to the Reverend, and that her children are called Adam and Olivia. Soon after, Nettie runs away from her and Celie's father, and Celie suggests that she should go stay with the Reverend and his wife. When she leaves,

Nettie tells Celie that she will write to her, and that the only thing that would stop her doing so is death. When no letters come, Celie concludes that her sister is dead, and she is left alone with Mr and his children. Mr is abusive towards Celie and leaves all the work around the house and in the fields to her. He is also in love with Shug Avery, a renowned jazz singer who appears sporadically in his life.

Harpo, one of Mr's sons, who works with Celie in the fields, impregnates and marries a girl named Sofia. He is unhappy at how strong-willed Sofia is, as she does not allow him to order her about or dominate her like his father does to Celie. Celie advises him to beat her but is surprised when she fights back. Sofia confronts Celie, who confesses that she only told Harpo to beat her because she is jealous of her. They make up and Sofia encourages Celie to stand up to Mr.

CELIE FALLS IN LOVE

One day, Celie and Mr hear rumours that Shug is ill. He brings her back to the house, and Celie nurses her back to health, with the two of them becoming friends in the process. We discover that Mr wishes that he had married Shug and not Celie, but Celie does not mind, and it becomes clear that she loves Shug herself.

While Shug is staying with them, Sofia becomes tired of Harpo's attempts to dominate her, so she takes their children and leaves him. After she leaves, Harpo opens a 'juke joint' near the house, where Shug sings for people every weekend. Now that she is better, Shug thinks about leaving, but stays when Celie tells her that Mr beats her. Some time later, we hear that Sofia has been brutally beaten by police and thrown in jail after getting into a fight with the mayor, whose wife wanted Sofia to become her maid. Celie goes to visit her and finds her to be losing her mind in prison. It is three years before Sofia is let out, on the condition that she must work as the mayor's maid after all. The family make Sofia sleep in their storeroom, and only allow her to see her children on rare occasions, leading her to liken her employment to slavery.

After some time, Shug returns, surprising Celie and Mr with her new husband, Grady. Despite this, Celie and Shug become increasingly intimate, and their relationship turns sexual. Shug asks Celie about her sister, Nettie, and on investigation, the two find out that she is not dead, but that Mr has been hiding her letters to Celie for many years. They find the letters in his trunk, and Nettie's story is revealed over the course of the letters.

NETTIE'S LETTERS

In the letters, we learnt that after leaving Celie, Nettie stayed with the reverend and his wife, named Samuel and Corrine, and their two adopted children (who are Celie's, though only she knows it). Nettie accompanies them and the children to Africa to carry out missionary work in a small rural village. Corrine is suspicious of Nettie's relationship with Samuel, thinking that she is the real mother of the two adopted children because they look so much like her. However, Samuel explains the situation, and we find out that Celie and Nettie's real father was lynched by white people soon after they were born, and that the man who raped Celie and fathered the two children is therefore not her father, but her stepfather. Nettie reveals to them that Celie is the mother of the two children just before Corrine dies from a long-term illness.

CELIE'S LIFE CHANGES

Although Celie is relieved that her children were not born from incest, on comprehending the full tragedy of her life, she questions whether God cares about her at all and begins to address her letters to Nettie instead. She decides to leave Mr, and goes with Shug and Grady to live in Shug's house in Memphis. Celie finds work making trousers, and is happier than she has ever been, for the first time enjoying money, friends and a meaningful relationship (with Shug). She is heartbroken, however, when Shug leaves her to pursue one last fling with a younger man. Shug tells Celie that she loves her and that she will return soon, and Celie goes to live in the house that she has inherited from her now dead step-father. Soon after, she is devastated on receiving a telegram telling her that Nettie has drowned en route back to America, along with a bundle of her letters unopened and unread. Nevertheless, we continue to see Nettie's letters to Celie.

NETTIE'S LETTERS

The village in Africa that Nettie has been living in for many years is destroyed by people from the city building a road, and she goes with the widowed Samuel and the children to England to seek help. They find none, but Nettie and Samuel realise that they love each other and marry before returning to Africa. On their return, they find that many of the villagers have left the destroyed village to seek out a group of runaways who are said to live deep in the forest. Adam announces his plans to marry one of the villagers, and they all decide to return to America together.

REUNION

In Shug's absence, Celie finds companionship with Mr, who has changed since she left him, and they talk mainly about their mutual love of Shug. Celie's trouser-making business expands, and she hires Sofia, who has after many years been allowed to leave the mayor and his wife's employment, and Mr to help. Celie has found contentment in her middle-age and is even happier when Shug returns to her, having been left by the younger man. In Celie's final letter, addressed to God, Nettie returns, and Celie is overjoyed to find out that she and her children are not dead.

CHARACTER STUDY

CELIE

Celie is often described as skinny and ugly, but she is deeply kind, creative and loyal to the people that she loves. She is the sister of Nettie, the mother of Adam and Olivia and the wife of Mr. She is oppressed by the men in her life (her husband and step-father) and as a result rightfully mistrusts them. She instead finds comfort in her relationships with women, in terms of both friendship and sex. These strong women help her to grow in confidence and refuse to accept the abusive treatment she receives from her husband. Celie is also defined in the novel through her relationship to God, to whom she addresses many of her letters. She sees God as male and sees his apparent indifference to her problems as typical of the men in her life. It is only through Shug, with whom she has a deep and intimate relationship, that she comes to see God as something more abstract.

SHUG

Shug is initially described as a beautiful and mysterious jazz singer, known only for her romantic relationship with Celie's husband, Mr. At first, she is cold and callous towards Celie, but as the two become close friends and lovers she is revealed to be a generous and warm person who loves life. She is open about her passion for the carnal and is judged by some for her love of sex and drink, telling Celie "one thing my mama hated me for was how much I love to fuck" (p. 115). She and Celie develop a deep and intimate relationship, and she helps Celie discover her sexuality, while also openly talking of how much she enjoys sex with men. She sees herself as a sinner but believes that God is in everything and everyone and has created the good things in life for people to enjoy and appreciate. She is strong-willed, free-spirited and impulsive, "bound to live her life and be herself no matter what" (p. 228), as Celie claims. She has lived the high life and towards the end of the novel feels herself getting old.

NETTIE

Nettie, Celie's younger sister, is defined by her passion for education. Unlike Celie, she escapes the trap of marriage, and pursues her education along with missionary work in Africa. She is kind and nurturing to Corrine and Samuel's children (who are actually her niece and nephew) and to the villagers in Africa and keeps up writing letters to her sister without reply for decades. Her passion for learning also fills in much historical context relating to the American slave trade, and many of her letters are highly anthropological, describing to Celie the origins of the slave trade in Africa and the differences between American and African society. After Corrine's death, she realises that she is in love with Samuel and the two marry happily. The book is shaped by Nettie's deep relationship with Celie, which is expressed through letters, many of which are not even read.

MR

Mr is an older man who is deeply in love with Shug Avery. He is lazy and physically and mentally abusive towards Celie when they are living together, and Celie believes this is because he wishes he had married Shug instead of her. He also tries to rape Nettie when she runs away from home, but she escapes. Despite his dark, violent side, Shug still loves him and sees the good in him. The two continue their affair when Shug comes to visit, but when she finds out that he beats his wife and has been hiding Nettie's letters she persuades Celie to come and live with her. After Celie deserts him, something seems to change in him. He does all the housework, works in the fields and seems to become kinder and more reflective when talking to Celie. Towards the end of the novel, this change allows him and Celie to become friends, united in their love of Shug, and he seems less bitter about his not having married her and just glad of the fact that he has loved and been loved.

SOFIA

Sofia marries Mr's son Harpo after he gets her pregnant. She is strong-willed and refuses to submit to Harpo's attempts to dominate her, leaving him and telling Celie that "he don't want a wife, he want a dog" (p. 58). Sofia is an important figure in the novel because it is through her that racial tensions in early 20th-century America are addressed, when she is beaten, thrown in jail and forced to work for the white mayor's family in conditions not dissimilar to slavery. She can be seen as a tragic character because her fierce will and desire to be free are stifled by the historical prejudices against her race and gender and she suffers greatly for her unwillingness to bend to the wills of others.

ANALYSIS

FORM AND STYLE

The Color Purple is an epistolary novel, told through the exchange of letters. The plot is therefore revealed to us through Celie and Nettie's correspondence. As a result, we know only what Celie and Nettie themselves know, and the novel is largely centred around their inner thoughts and feelings, rather than lengthy descriptions of the setting, characters or historical context. The plot is framed through the remembrances of major incidents concerning the two sisters and their family and friends, which means that it is often fragmented. There is little mapping out of timings either, as we are not told how long has passed between each letter.

The epistolary form also means that the novel is written in the style of the letter-writers, each of whom have their own particular characteristics. For example, Celie has not been afforded the privilege of an extensive education, and so her letters are highly colloquial and written using non-standard English, while Nettie's are far more formal, reflecting her own education.

HISTORICAL CONTEXT

Though the novel spans two decades, it primarily takes place during the 1930s, in the American South and in Africa. Most of its characters, at least on Celie's side, are African-Americans, and the racism of American society at the time is often noticeable. Slavery in America had been abolished less than a hundred years ago, and the lingering prejudices and Jim Crow laws, which imposed racial segregation in the South of the country, made it near impossible for many African-Americans to better their socio-economic position. This situation was made worse by the violent hostility shown by many white Americans, and we can see this reflected in the novel, with Celie's father being lynched by white people and Sofia being brutally beaten, imprisoned and forced into slave-like employment for standing up to a white woman.

The period was also characterised by the repression of women, who were often forced into marriage and motherhood against their will, and expected to raise the children, keep the house and suffer the domination of their fathers and husbands. The novel follows Celie as she breaks free of the oppressive male relationships in her life.

Towards the novel's final stages, at the end of the 1930s and the start of the 1940s, there are also hints at the presence of the Second World War, which raged throughout Europe, Asia and Africa from 1939 to 1945. Celie thinks that Nettie has been killed by German mines on the way back to America but is proved wrong by her return.

MAJOR THEMES

Conception of God

Much of the novel, and indeed its title, explores the theme of religion, and more specifically the concept of God. To Celie, God has always been a white man, "the god I been praying and writing to is a man" and as such seems to reflect the other males in her life: "And act just like all the other mens I know", causing her to wonder whether God cares about her at all (p. 164). It is through her relationships with Shug and Nettie that her viewpoint shifts and she is shown different conceptions of the divine. Shug sees God in a far more spiritual way, through the beauty of nature. She sees God in "everything" and inside each person, not as a he or a she, but an "it" (p. 167). She sees the pleasurable, surprising and beautiful things in life ("the color purple in a field") as God's attempts to please (*ibid.*). This spiritualism is reflected in Nettie's account of the African village in which she does missionary work. For the villagers, and for Nettie, God is internal and spiritual and can be seen in everything rather than being fixed, as in the popular Western conception of God as a white, bearded man. As she says to Celie in one of her letters, "not being tied to what God looks like, frees us" (p. 218).

Sexuality

Though never overtly discussed, homosexuality is an important theme in *The Color Purple*, as explored in Celie's romantic and sexual relationship with Shug. Celie's first sexual experiences come in the form of rape by her step-father, and to begin with she has sex solely for her husband's pleasure and for reproduction. She admits to Shug that she has never enjoyed sex before. Given that she becomes pregnant twice in just the first few pages of the novel, it is no wonder that she associates sex with pain, discomfort and the indignity of unwanted pregnancy. It is through meeting Shug that Celie discovers her own sexuality and learns to enjoy sex. Shug is clearly attracted to people of both genders, and through her relationship with Celie, she teaches her the ins and outs of her body, falling into a deeply intimate relationship in the process. Though her sexuality is never explicitly defined in the novel, it is clear that Celie's relationships with women are far more fulfilling to her than those with men. This goes beyond sexuality, as the emotional intimacy that she shares with Nettie, her friends and Shug is far greater than that she shared with her husband.

A comparison of cultures

Nettie's descriptions of her time at the Olinka village in Africa can be compared with Celie's own narrative set in the American South to give insight into the differences and similarities between the two societies. Nettie goes to Africa as a missionary, expecting to bring 'civilised' Western culture and religion to rural African communities, but we find out that certain social injustices in the village resemble those in America. In one letter, Nettie laments the fact that girls are not educated: "The Olinka do not believe girls should be educated. When I asked a mother why she thought this, she said: A girl is nothing to herself; only to her husband can she become something" (p. 132).

While perhaps more extreme, we can see that this resembles Celie's own situation in America, as she is taken out of school at the age of 14 to marry an older man and look after his children. No importance is given to her own life, and just like with the Olinka, her husband's needs are seen as the priority. Indeed, Nettie goes on to see the similarities that this oppression of women has with the treatment of African-Americans back home, when Olivia tells her: "They're like white people at home who don't want colored people to learn" (p. 133).

Walker shows that systematic oppression crosses societal boundaries, a crossing which is reflected in the diaspora of African-Americans resulting from the American slave trade.

FURTHER REFLECTION

SOME QUESTIONS TO THINK ABOUT...

- How does Walker show the effects of racism in the American South in the novel?
- In what ways would Celie's life have been different if she was a man?
- Compare Celie's relationship with Shug to her relationship with her husband, Mr. In what ways are they different?
- Why does Celie think of God as a white man? How do her conception of God and her attitude towards religion change throughout the novel?
- The story is told through a series of letters. How would the novel be different if letters had not been used?
- How does the society of the Olinka in Africa differ from American society, and how is it similar?
- Examine the way that Celie changes throughout the novel. How do the people around her influence her?

- How does the novel challenge traditional gender roles? How do the men in the novel treat the women around them?
- In what way does the film adaptation to *The Color Purple* differ from the book?

We want to hear from you!
Leave a comment on your online library
and share your favourite books on social media!

FURTHER READING

REFERENCE EDITION

- Walker, A. (1995) *The Color Purple*. London: The Women's Press Ltd.

REFERENCE STUDIES

- The Editors of Encyclopaedia Britannica (2018) Alice Walker. *Encyclopaedia Britannica*. [Online]. [Accessed 2 September 2018]. Available from: <https://www.britannica.com/biography/Alice-Walker>

ADDITIONAL SOURCES

- Gates, H. L. and Appiah, A. (1993) *Alice Walker: Critical Perspectives Past and Present*. New York: Amistad.

- Walker, A. (1988) *Living by the Word: Selected Writings 1973-1987*. London: The Women's Press Ltd.

ADAPTATIONS

- *The Color Purple*. (1985) [Film]. Steven Spielberg. Dir. USA: Warner Bros.

www.brightsummaries.com

Ebook EAN: 9782808012201

Paperback EAN: 9782808012218

Legal Deposit: D/2018/12603/358

Cover: © Primento

Digital conception by Primento, the digital partner of
publishers.

Printed by Amazon Italia Logistica S.r.l.
Torrazza Piemonte (TO), Italy

23100573R00027